MW01248516

GRANDPA & Me

from you to me®

Grandpa & Me will take you on an interactive and fun journey, having a great time getting to know each other better.

Tips to enjoy Grandpa & Me :

- Your questions are in gold. Grandpa's questions are in grey.
- Dip in and complete your questions in any order, whenever you want.
- Use words, drawings, doodles . . . whatever feels right for you.
- There are no right or wrong answers, just your own.
- Use the extra pages to capture anything else you would like to explore.
- Agree when and how to share your pages with the other person.
- Enjoy yourself and have fun!

A bit about Grandpa . . .

My full name :

My age : Today's Date :

A picture of Grandpa . . . a drawing or photo

A bit about Me . . .

My full name :

My age : Today's date :

A picture of Me . . . a drawing or photo

A bit about Grandpa . . .

What I love watching on television :

Best movies :

Top songs :

Favorite places :

Things I say a lot :

I love to eat :

A bit about Me . . .

What I love watching on television :

Best movies :

Top songs :

Favorite places :

Things I say a lot :

I love to eat :

Today . . .

Who I talked to :

What I did :

The best things :

The worst things :

What I wanted to do, but didn't get around to :

GRANDPA

Today . . .

Who I talked to :

What I did :

The best things :

The worst things :

What I wanted to do, but didn't get around to :

When I was younger . . .

My earliest memory :

What I was like :

When I was younger I thought that :

When I was younger . . .

My earliest memory :

What I was like :

When I was younger I thought that :

Happened to me . . .

Funny things :

Embarrassing things :

Sad things :

Happened to me . . .

Funny things :

Embarrassing things :

Sad things :

The way we are . . .

The ways we are similar :

The ways we are different :

Things I admire about you :

The way we are . . .

The ways we are similar :

The ways we are different :

Things I admire about you :

My family . . .

Some great memories of our family :

What I love about our family :

What I would like to be different :

My family . . .

Some great memories of our family :

What I love about our family :

What I would like to be different :

Family times . . .

Things I love doing with my family :

I wish we could :

I wish we didn't :

Family times . . .

Things I love doing with my family :

I wish we could :

I wish we didn't :

Where I live . . .

What I remember about the places I have lived :

Things at home that are special :

Where I might like to live in the future :

Where I live . . .

What I remember about the places I have lived :

Things at home that are special :

Where I might like to live in the future :

Birthdays . . .

My best memories :

How I would like to spend future birthdays :

My perfect present would be :

Birthdays . . .

My best memories :

How I would like to spend future birthdays :

My perfect present would be :

Vacations . . .

My best memories :

The best places I have been :

Where I would love to visit :

Vacations . . .

My best memories :

The best places I have been :

Where I would love to visit :

With friends . . .

How I feel about my friends :

What I admire most about you and your friends :

What I want to change about my friendships :

With friends . . .

How I feel about my friends :

What I admire most about you and your friends :

What I want to change about my friendships :

Messages for my friends . . .

Messages for my friends . . .

My Spare time . . .

What I enjoy doing most in my spare time :

What I would love to do :

What I love watching you do :

My Spare time . . .

What I enjoy doing most in my spare time :

What I would love to do :

What I love you watching me do :

School . . .

What I loved about being at school :

What I found most difficult :

With the benefit of hindsight :

School . . .

What I love about being at school :

What I find most difficult :

My greatest learning experience :

Learning . . .

What I would love to learn :

How I best like to learn :

The help I would like from you :

Learning . . .

What I would love to learn :

How I best like to learn :

The help I would like from you :

Me

Books & Stories . . .

Some of my favorite books :

Books I love that I hope you will read :

Books I would love to read :

Books & Stories . . .

Some of my favorite books :

Favorite characters from my books :

Books I would love to read :

Some of my favorite things . . .

GRANDPA

Some of my favorite things . . .

Me

Growing up . . .

What was exciting :

What I was concerned about :

The help and guidance I received :

Growing up . . .

What is exciting :

What I am concerned about :

The help I would like :

My body . . .

How I feel about me :

What I like about me :

What I would like to share with you :

My body . . .

How I feel about me :

What I like about me :

What I would like to share with you :

Being healthy . . .

A drawing of my ideas to be fit and healthy :

Being healthy . . .

A drawing of my ideas to be fit and healthy :

Feeling happy . . .

The things that make me happy :

What makes me feel confident :

Who I love spending time with :

Feeling happy . . .

The things that make me happy :

What makes me feel confident :

Who I love spending time with :

Feeling Sad . . .

The things that make me sad :

What knocks my confidence :

What helps me when I feel sad :

Feeling Sad . . .

The things that make me sad :

What shakes my confidence :

What helps me when I feel sad :

My Worries . . .

Things that worry me :

Some of my regrets :

How I best manage any worries :

My worries . . .

Things that worry me :

Some of my regrets :

How I best manage any worries :

Falling in love . . .

My views on love :

What is important to me :

My first love and what I learned :

Falling in love . . .

My views on love :

What is important to me :

What I have learnt so far :

My future . . .

Things I want to do in my life :

Things I want to do with you :

Some words to describe the person I want to be :

My future . . .

Things I want to do in my life :

Things I want to do with you :

Some words to describe the person I want to be :

My dreams . . .

What I dream about :

How I see my future :

What I wish I could spend more time doing :

My dreams . . .

What I dream about :

How I see my future :

What I wish I could spend more time doing :

Grandpa & Me . . .

What I love about you :

What I love about us :

What I wish we could do more of :

Me & Grandpa . . .

What I love about you :

What I love about us :

What I wish we could do more of :

Thoughts I have . . .

In 5 years :

I hope :

Something you don't know about me :

GRANDPA

Thoughts I have . . .

In 5 years :

I hope :

Something you don't know about me :

Helping others . . .

People I admire who help others :

How I like to help others :

What I could do more :

Helping others . . .

People I admire who help others :

How I like to help others :

What I could do more :

Topics of Grandpa's choice . . .

These pages are for you, Grandpa, to write questions . . .

Topics of Grandpa's choice . . .

. . . or topics for you and your child to answer

Topics of my choice . . .

These pages are for you to write questions . . .

Topics of my choice . . .

. . . or topics for you and your Grandpa to answer

A poem about me & you . . .

A poem about me & you . . .

A letter to myself based on what I have discovered in this journal . . .

Dear Me

A letter to myself based on what I have discovered in this journal . . .

Dear Me

Thinking about what I have discovered from this journal, here is a picture showing my dreams for the future . . .

Thinking about what I have discovered from this journal, here is a picture showing my dreams for the future . . .

Final thoughts & doodles . . .

Final thoughts & doodles . . .

GRANDPA & Me

First published in the USA by *from you to me* February 2015.
Copyright from you to me limited 2015
ISBN 978-1-907048-68–5

Printed and bound in China by Imago.
This paper is manufactured from pulp sourced from forests that are legally and sustainably managed.

For more information please contact:
from you to me ltd
The Old Brewery
Newtown
Bradford on Avon
BA15 1NF, UK

hello@fromyoutome.com
www.fromyoutome.com

All rights reserved. No part of this publication may be reproduced, stored in a retrieval system or transmitted in any form or by any means, electronic, mechanical, photocopying or otherwise circulated without the publisher's prior consent in any form of binding or cover other than that in which it is published and without a similar condition including this.

Published by *from you to me* ltd

All titles are available at good gift and book stores or www.fromyoutome.com

from you to me Journals of a Lifetime

Dear Mom
Dear Dad
Dear Grandma
Dear Grandpa
Dear Sister
Dear Brother
Dear Daughter
Dear Son
Dear Friend

Parent & Child

Bump to Birthday, pregnancy & first year journal
Our Story, for my daughter
Our Story, for my son
Dear Baby, guest book
Early Years, birth to five years journal

Get Kids Writing

Mom & Me
Dad & Me
Grandma & Me
Grandpa & Me

Other Titles

Love Stories, anniversary & relationship journal
Cooking up Memories

Many of these journals can be personalized online at www.fromyoutome.com